TRACTORS
1939 John Deere Model H, Columbia County, Oregon

BROWNTROUT PUBLISHERS • SAN FRANCISCO, CALIFORNIA

TRACTORS
Farmall tractor, green and white barn, Harvard, Illinois

PUBLISHED BY BROWNTROUT • SAN FRANCISCO, CALIFORNIA

TRACTORS
1927 Case, Herc Bouris, owner, Menifee, California

PUBLISHED BY BROWNTROUT • SAN FRANCISCO, CALIFORNIA

TRACTORS
Ford Model 8N, Columbia County, Oregon

PUBLISHED BY BROWNTROUT • SAN FRANCISCO, CALIFORNIA

TRACTORS
International 966, Westminster, Maryland

PUBLISHED BY BROWNTROUT • SAN FRANCISCO, CALIFORNIA

TRACTORS
1954 Super W-6 McCormick-Deering International,
Jim Schilling, owner, Great Falls, Montana

PUBLISHED BY BROWNTROUT • SAN FRANCISCO, CALIFORNIA

TRACTORS
Wards tractor and hay barn, Indiana

PUBLISHED BY BROWNTROUT • SAN FRANCISCO, CALIFORNIA

TRACTORS
1950s Case tractor, Buena Vista, California

PUBLISHED BY BROWNTROUT • SAN FRANCISCO, CALIFORNIA

TRACTORS
John Deere 700, northern California

PUBLISHED BY BROWNTROUT • SAN FRANCISCO, CALIFORNIA

TRACTORS
Old Ford tractor and firewood, Royalston, Massachusetts

PUBLISHED BY BROWNTROUT • SAN FRANCISCO, CALIFORNIA

TRACTORS
Farmall tractor and square barn, Camas Prairie,
Grangeville, Idaho

PUBLISHED BY BROWNTROUT • SAN FRANCISCO, CALIFORNIA

TRACTORS
1938 Case RC, Tom Railsback, owner, Great Falls, Montana

PUBLISHED BY BROWNTROUT • SAN FRANCISCO, CALIFORNIA

TRACTORS
Blue Ford with hot air balloon

PUBLISHED BY BROWNTROUT • SAN FRANCISCO, CALIFORNIA

TRACTORS
Massey Ferguson, red barn, Chambers County, Alabama

PUBLISHED BY BROWNTROUT • SAN FRANCISCO, CALIFORNIA

TRACTORS
C. 1920 Fordson and McCormick tractors and plow,
San Andreas, California

PUBLISHED BY BROWNTROUT • SAN FRANCISCO, CALIFORNIA

TRACTORS
Case at Greenstone Winery, Amador County, California

PUBLISHED BY BROWNTROUT • SAN FRANCISCO, CALIFORNIA

TRACTORS
#11 Allis-Chalmers tractor, San Joaquin County, California

PUBLISHED BY BROWNTROUT • SAN FRANCISCO, CALIFORNIA

TRACTORS
"Vigneron 60," woodshed, San Joaquin County, California

PUBLISHED BY BROWNTROUT • SAN FRANCISCO, CALIFORNIA

TRACTORS
John Deere collection, eastern Washington

PUBLISHED BY BROWNTROUT • SAN FRANCISCO, CALIFORNIA

TRACTORS
C. 1915 Case steam tractor, Nut Tree, California

PUBLISHED BY BROWNTROUT • SAN FRANCISCO, CALIFORNIA

TRACTORS
1948 Farmall Model MD Diesel, Gary Larsen, owner,
Great Falls, Montana

PUBLISHED BY BROWNTROUT • SAN FRANCISCO, CALIFORNIA

TRACTORS
A BOOK OF 21 POSTCARDS

BROWNTROUT PUBLISHERS
SAN FRANCISCO • CALIFORNIA

BROWNTROUT PUBLISHERS

P.O. BOX 280070
SAN FRANCISCO • CALIFORNIA 94128-0070

ISBN: 1-56313-786-0
TITLE #: P6786

BROWNTROUT publishes a large line of calendars, photographic books, and postcard books.
Please write for more information.